Contents

Aboriginal Culture & Art Style Regions

Map of the Pacific Northwest Coast

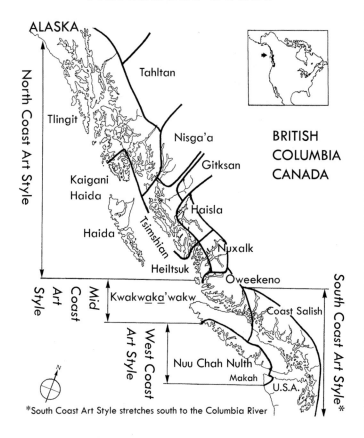

ALASKA

North Coast Art Style

Tahltan

Tlingit

Nisga'a

BRITISH
COLUMBIA
CANADA

Gitksan

Kaigani
Haida

Haisla

Haida

Tsimshian

Nuxalk

Heiltsuk

Oweekeno

Kwakwaka'wakw

Coast Salish

South Coast Art Style *

North Coast Art Style

Mid Coast Art Style

West Coast Art Style

Nuu Chah Nulth

Makah

U.S.A.

*South Coast Art Style stretches south to the Columbia River

Along the Pacific Northwest Coast, from Alaska through British Columbia to Washington, there are several related, yet diverse, aboriginal cultures (First Nations). The map shows the general geographic areas, with their rugged shorelines, dense forests, and steep mountains, rich in natural resources.

Prior to contact with Europeans, these peoples had developed complex social systems, wide trade routes, economic prosperity, and one of the most complex art forms in the world. Just after contact, before the new and deadly imported diseases took their terrible toll on every single village, there was a surge in wealth and art production.

Today, a newcomer to this world of art and culture may well ask, "What am I seeing when I look at Pacific Northwest Coast aboriginal art?" You are seeing the

The Potlatch

result of thousands of years of tradition and skill development.

The Potlatch (traditional First Nations business) and the Winter Ceremonies were the main reasons for which masks and ceremonial regalia such as button blankets, Chilkat dancing blankets, paddle shirts or dancing shawls, as well as decorated containers to store wealth, jewelry, gifts and all manner of related objects and art were, and still are, created.

On reserves, in museums, in public spaces, and in the art, you may see the family Bighouses or Longhouses decorated inside and out to display family history, origin stories, status and wealth. You may see canoes, those containers of souls for sea or spirit voyages. You may also see the large totem poles, which tell the stories and histories of a family or clan through carved images.

For three seasons of the year, they worked long arduous days hunting, gathering and preserving food, but in the long, dark hours of winter, aboriginal people gathered together to feed their souls and to nourish their spirits. As the spirit world neared the earth, it was time to listen, to tell stories and histories, to sing legends, to dance origin myths and to be initiated into societies. Relations and friends would come from far and near to witness together at the Potlatches, feasts and Winter Ceremonies.

Often there would be hundreds of witnesses to marriage investments, settlements, paying back of debts, gain or loss of social rank, and enforcement of rules and protocol so that the tribe could be proud of its members. Also, combined as it was with singing, dancing and theatrical entertainment, the Potlatch was an exciting and pleasurable way to spend the winter months.

The objective of the giver of the Potlatch was to give away as much property as possible to all who attended to witness the event. Anyone who received a gift was, in effect, given a loan that must be returned plus 25% - 100% interest. A young person was given his first blankets by the tribe so that he could lend these to others, receive interest, pay his debts and develop credit.

It was honourable to amass a fortune, not for oneself, but to give away at a great potlatch. Nowadays, ceremony and display is still a hallmark of the Potlatch, providing to all who come a bridge between the contemporary world and the traditional culture.

The following pages are organized as an alphabetical reference. The book is divided into three sections: three-dimensional objects, creature/being designs and design components. Included within these sections are objects you might expect to see within traditional and contemporary First Nations cultures as well as commonly depicted creatures.

You will learn how to identify a design, whether you see it in a painting, an engraved piece of jewelry or as a carved mask or totem pole figure.

To clarify: when "the art" is mentioned, it means the aboriginal art from the Pacific Northwest Coast. Creatures' names that are capitalized refer to

their spirit ancestor. For example, "Beaver" refers to the spirit animal/person instead of "the beaver." The terms "aboriginal" and "First Nations" refer respectfully to the descendents of the original people to inhabit the Pacific Northwest Coast.

Variations of design, story, history and meaning are found within each of the traditional First Nations. Of necessity, explanations in this book are incomplete and do not always apply to every culture.

This little guide book, designed to give you a mere glimpse of Pacific Northwest Coast art, hopes to lead you to a deeper understanding and whet your appetite for learning more about today's vibrant, complex aboriginal cultures.

Unless otherwise noted, all two-dimensional designs are the original artwork of Jim Gilbert. Realistic scenes are by Karin Clark. Illustrations and adaptations of original First Nations (aboriginal) carvings are by Karin Clark.

Potlatch Pole

Materials Used by Aboriginal Artists

Traditionally, aboriginal artists from the Pacific Northwest Coast used the following materials: antlers, bark, beaks (puffin), bone and other animal parts, claws, copper, feathers, fur, grasses, hides, hooves from deer and mountain goats, horns from mountain goats and mountain sheep, ivory from walrus tusks, oils, paints, quills from porcupines, roots from spruce and cedar trees, shells from abalone, mussels, clams, operculum from moon snails, dentalia shells, skulls, argillite slate from the Haida region, stones such as nephrite (jade) or obsidian, teeth from bears, stains, wool from dogs and mountain goats, wood from mainly yellow and red cedar trees, but also, alder, birch, hemlock, maple, spruce, and yew.

After contact with Europeans, artists used: steel tools, beads from North American, European, and Russian traders, commercially made blankets and woollen cloth, mother-of-pearl buttons, commercially made paint, canvas, paper, glass, silver and gold, cast bronze, semi-precious and precious stones, pottery and lately, computer graphics and multi-media.

Paint

Black paint pigment was carbon from such things as wood charcoal, soot, lignite or graphite. Red was ground hematite, cinnabar, or various ochres. Green or blue/green was made by mixing ground copper minerals, sulphide of copper, copper oxides or blue mineralized clay. White came from burnt clam shells ground to a fine powder with a stone mortar and pestle, then mixed with a binder. Binders could be saliva, dried salmon roe, water and various kinds of oils.

Later, dry powdered pigments such as Chinese vermilion, verdigris (green), Reckitts blue, as well as graphite and powdered red lead from ships' stores were popular trade items.

Paint Colour Symbolism

Black and red paints may represent death, while red signifies life and sacrifice or birth. Perhaps black represents the form-giving womb or Mother Earth. The formline of most Northwest Coast art is black. The red might be blood, or inner life. Inner secondary shapes are usually red. The white, or negative, spaces between the black and red can represent wind, spirit, or air.

Three Dimensional Objects

Bentwood Boxes

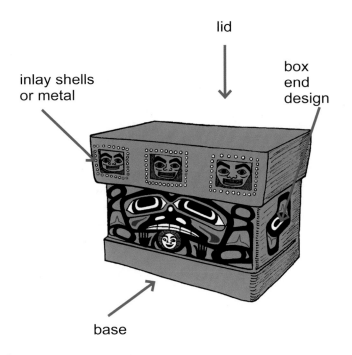

lid

box end design

inlay shells or metal

base

Bentwood Box With Ornate Design

For many First Nations coastal groups, the sacred shape was a rectangle or box, and the sacred number was four. The Nisga'a believed boxes contained souls and wealth.

They entered the box of the world, slept in a cradle box, perhaps sat in a chief's seat, a three-sided box turned inside out. They were sustained by the food cooked and stored in their boxes. Tools, regalia, masks and other precious wealth was stored in the boxes. After death, a high-ranking individual's remains might be placed in a grave box.

Prior to contact and previous to metal tools, aboriginal craftsmen split a single plank from a cedar or spruce tree. All four sides were, and are still, made from this single piece of wood, kerfed (grooved or notched), steamed, bent, rounded on three corners, and pinned with wooden pegs on the fourth. This last seam may have also been drilled and tied with cedar withes. A bottom was fitted inside. On some boxes, a top was carved so that it fit over the sides.

Boxes could contain wealth or ceremonial objects, household goods, food, or fishing and hunting gear. Women would place fire-heated rocks in the water contained by lidless boxes and cook in them.

To increase the value of the box, the artist decorated it with painting, shallow relief carving, shells, or metal to illustrate stories or crests. Decorated boxes might be so important that they had their own names.

Cooking in Bentwood Boxes

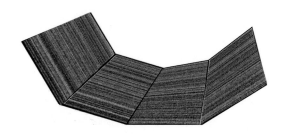

Plank laid out, with grooves, partially bent

Bighouses (Longhouses)

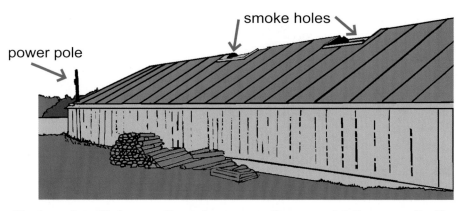

smoke holes

power pole

Modern-day Bighouse (Longhouse, or Ceremonial Community House)

Along the coast, several related families lived together in a large rectangular house made out of red cedar. A massive tree, the red cedar made it possible for the builders to cut and use the huge posts and beams that held plank roofs and walls, also split from the straight-grained cedar tree. The houses came to be called BIghouses or Longhouses because of their size and shape.

Floors were dirt with cedar mats covering sitting or sleeping areas. Woven cedar mats divided the living areas. Fire pits were in the centre and in the cooking areas. Adjustable smoke holes let the smoke escape through the roof.

Very large houses could accommodate hundreds of guests and some had rectangular stages or sunken dance areas.

House chiefs had the highest ranking within the house. The village chief was usually the wealthiest of the house chiefs. House sites and house names were a valuable part of the economy. When a new house was built, a Potlatch would be held to acknowledge the owner's increased status in front of witnesses.

Historically, communities lived in permanent winter villages but moved to various food gathering

House Front

Kwakwaka'wakw house front design showing Thunderbird helping to build the first Bighouse at the Nimpkish River by lifting and placing the large roof beams with his talons.

House Post

Bill Helin

areas during the seasons. House skeletons (posts and beams) were left behind in these summer areas. By taking the planks for the walls and roof with them from the winter village, the people were able to quickly set up a summer village.

Housefronts could be decorated with paintings or relief carvings. Entrances were small, round, oval or rectangular, providing protection from bad weather. Visitors had to bend to enter. Therefore, an enemy would be at a disadvantage. The head chiefs might have sculpted poles, now called totem poles, that would depict lineages, crests and family stories. Sometimes mortuary or memorial poles flanked the main pole, depicting ancestry stories or holding remains.

Large house posts, cut from a single tree, often carved and painted, held up the enormous roof beams of traditional Longhouses and Bighouses. The top figure of the post held the beams on its head.

Builders of many contemporary Big-houses, or ceremonial community houses, still use the large post and beam construction style of their ancestors.

Button Blankets

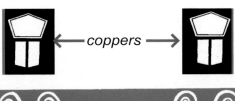

coppers

Breaching Whale Button Blanket with Wave Motifs

Today. button blankets usually have a dark navy, green or black background with red appliquéed crests and designs on them. These designs and trim often have hundreds of decorative buttons sewn on them. Earlier, these buttons were made of abalone and mother of pearl but now are frequently made of plastic. Bells, shells, hooves and other ornaments are sometimes attached to the dancing aprons worn under the blankets.

Much of the Northwest Coast art depicts family crests. Like some present-day trademarks and the crests of old Europe, First Nations' crests express and record the ancestry, rank and privileges of the person, clan or family, as well as historical relationships between clans.

Most clans have stories of how their supernatural

At a Modern-day Potlatch

far away, war, or a when member had an extraordinary vision. The family would hold a potlatch and introduce the new crest. Their guests would witness and acknowledge the new crest.

On the blankets you can see crests that are humans, plants, animals, objects, aspects of the environment like the sun, moon or stars, and mythical beings or combinations of these things.

or partly human ancestor at the beginning of time fought a battle with a supernatural creature. The descendents of that ancestor inherit the right to create and dance a mask form of their ancestor and use their crests on objects and ceremonial regalia. Songs, stories and dances are also inherited.

Crests may be transferred through marriage, conquest, trade, reward for special services, or death of a lineage. New crests were created when families had special events, such as moving

Canoes

Canoe

Ravensong Canoe carved by Bill Helin and helpers

Traditionally, the coast people used canoes to travel because the high mountains and dense forests made land travel difficult. Depending on the culture and whether a canoe was used for fishing, hunting, whaling, war, trading, or making long sea voyages, it could be different styles and sizes. Some Haida canoes were up to 60 metres (180 feet) long. Aboriginal people respected and valued canoe builders.

Shamans, or medicine people, may search for wisdom or lost souls in a spirit canoe. A shaman's last journey from the living to the spirit world may be when his body is sent out to sea in a canoe.

Important canoes were given names. Explorers, visitors and settlers prized miniature and model canoes as souvenirs.

Coming Home from Food Gathering

Canoes in the art symbolize travel, a spiritual voyage, or containers for ideas.

Paddles were used to propel canoes, and to signal other travelers over long distances. Some were also designed to be used as fighting weapons.

The people would offer gifts to beings of the Undersea world from the blade of a paddle.

Paddle models may be used by dancers in certain dances, on shirts as ornaments that click when the wearer moves, as gifts, and as pieces of display art.

Bill Helin

Ravensong Canoe Photo

Hats

North Coast Crest Hat

three potlatch rings or skils

painted whale design

Hat Brim from Above

tail

fins

fins

head

men with harpoons

canoes with crew members

whales

line with floats

Nuu Chah Nulth Chief or Whaler's Hat

Coastal aboriginal people wore many kinds of hats or head gear and used many materials to make them. They wove headbands, conical hats, carved wooden helmets and frontlets, and used animal skin headdresses.

Some head coverings were use by shamans for sacred ceremonies. Some were practical, and provided protection from the sun and the endless coastal rains. Certain styles were reserved for high-ranking individuals. Painted or carved crests showed an owner's clan. A northern hat had a cylindrical tower on top of it, each segment of it called a skil. Each skil recorded a public ceremony which honoured the hat and its current owner.

A Nuu Chah Nulth whaling chief's hat was woven like a cone, topped with a bulbous dome and decorated with whaling images.

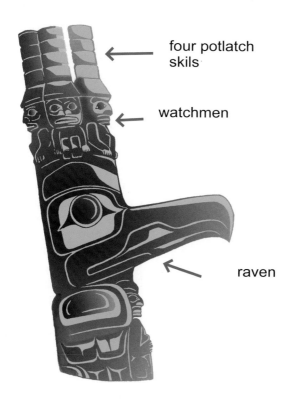

four potlatch skils

watchmen

raven

Potlatch Pole

The Watchmen on the top of this pole are guardians responsible for protecting the pole's owner's property and sometimes an entire village.

Facing several directions, they warn of approaching enemies or friends.

Sometimes there would be a single figure on the tops of the poles, but some poles had groups of two or three. Watchers wear conical hats, topped with rings, or skils, indicating the power and high status of the owner.

Jewelry / Adornment

Owl Bracelet

Bill Helin

Spirit Bear Magic

Split Eagle Bracelet

Traditionally, both men and women wore ornaments like earrings, finger rings, bracelets, anklets, neck rings, necklaces, pendants and belts. Women wore labrets (a disk implanted in the lower lip), and men wore nose rings or pins,

In the art, a bone nose pin may represent a shaman, and a labret shows a high-ranking woman.

Today, artists engrave or carve silver, gold, platinum, add precious and semi-precious stones creating many varieties of jewelry.

Earrings and Pendants

Engraved Eagle Earrings

Engraved Mid Coast Thunderbird Pendant

Bill designed this Moon Man medallion with all the elements of night life shining from his spirit for the Commonwealth Games in1994. The original gold Moon Man medallion with ruby eyes traveled in space on the Space Shuttle Columbia STS 78 in 1996.

Bill Helin

Moon Man Medallion

Masks

Cannibal Bird Mask

Today, as in historical times, many First Nations people believe that masks have spirit and identity. Traditional aboriginal artists first feel the spirit in the wood and then carve it to release the spirit's identity.

It is not so much that a dancer wears a mask to dance a story as s/he gives the mask legs so that it can tell its own story. First Nations people say they "dance the mask" and have many stories to tell about strange occurrences in the places where the masks are stored when they are not being danced.

Dancers may wear the masks over their faces, over their entire heads and in some cases, over much of their bodies. The entity of the mask confers knowledge, status and/or special powers to the human wearer when used in ceremony and ritual, both sacred and secular.

Wolf Dancer

A transformation mask is engineered to open, revealing one or two additional faces hidden underneath. In some cultures, relatives wear a mourning mask at a person's funeral, and the songs sung indicate that the person has now assumed the ancestral form. In other cultures, mourning masks commemorate those who have died in the past seasons.

In Kwakwa̱ka'wakw society, the winter ceremonial season's dances often initiate novices into secret dancing societies. The uninitiated in the village become the audience for the initiated and the novices.

In the Wolf dance, dancers wear wolf masks or frontlets, with cloth or fur backing. Sometimes a wolf plank mask sits just over the forehead and the face is showing.

Both men and women can dance the masks. The wolf-like movements and ritual turning, dipping and holding of hand positions typify this dance.

When the dancers begin, the Bighouse is lit with small spotlights and the large fire in the centre of the floor blazes. Drummers and singers vibrate the whole house and magic is in the air. Drummers may hold hide-covered drums in their hands and use beaters to mark the rhythm. In other cultures, the drum is a carved, hollow log with several drummers using sticks to sound the beat.

Mortuary Poles

Box-shaped flat frontal board

Mortuary Pole

Among some cultures, mortuary poles, with their distinctive box-front shapes on the top, were raised to honour a high-ranking man or woman. Relatives would place the cremated or reduced remains in the hollowed-out cavity on top of the pole behind the frontal board. The poles were placed with the butt side up to provide more space to make the hollow. Additional boards covered the remains, protecting them from the wind and weather.

The pole often had figures carved on the frontal board as well as the pole.

Some cultures simply raised memorial poles to honour their chiefs. They might have a single crest at the top, bottom or carved along the whole length of the pole.

Totem Poles

Artist Bill Helin working on the world's tallest totem pole*

Majestic monuments in cedar, each carved from a single tree trunk, sometimes with added beaks, wings or fins, totem poles were among the largest works created by Pacific Northwest Coast artists.

Poles had spirits and names. They were harvested with thanksgiving and ceremony, carved with ceremony, raised with ceremony and left to die like a living being.

The wealthier and high-ranking families had poles sculpted for them by master craftsmen. The wealth of resources allowed distinct professions to emerge and some people became masters at finding, cutting and transporting a pole to a carving place. Others might be masters at designing, carving and painting. These sculptures, now called totem poles, would display lineages, crests, and family stories. Sometimes mortuary or memorial poles flanked the main pole, depicting ancestry stories or holding remains.

Many of the totem poles were taken away or destroyed in the first half of the twentieth century, and the art of carving them fell into disuse. Due to the efforts of a few carvers who kept up their skills and passed those on to relatives, the art of carving has revived and flourished.

Some museums have had carvers duplicate or restore preserved totem poles so that the world can come to know and appreciate this amazing art and visual history form.

*The world's tallest totem pole, 54.94-m (180-ft 3-in) tall, known as the Spirit of Lekwammen ("Land of the Winds"), was raised on August 4, 1994 at Victoria, British Columbia, Canada prior to the Commonwealth Games taking place there. On August 26, 1997 the pole was partially dismantled for safety reasons.

Bill Helin

Queneesh and the Great Flood

that they were seeing Queneesh, the Whale Spirit, and that they would now be saved. The rain stopped, and the waters receded. Queneesh once again became the glacier. When the people see him, they are reminded to treat the Creator's gifts with respect and thankfulness.

Many aboriginal cultures from all over the world have stories about the Great Flood. Nations from around the Comox Valley in British Columbia tell the story of Queneesh, the Great White Whale spirit of the Comox Glacier.

Long ago, a chief was warned that the Creator was going to flood the world to wash away the people's betrayal of the earth. The valley people were to build many canoes and tie them with cedar bark to the top of the Glacier. When the rains came, the water climbed above the totem poles, up the side of the mountain and the Glacier itself was swallowed into the sea. The canoes filled with water and the people were being pulled into the ocean to drown. After they had tried everything to keep afloat, they prayed to the Great Creator. At that moment, the glacier slipped off the mountain and an enormous white whale breached above the water. The people knew

Beaver Eagle Pole

A totem pole carved from a single tree demands that the creatures and crest beings be vertical. Fins, wings, and beaks must sometimes be cut from a different piece of wood and attached later. These same body parts may be folded in, around, down, or up to conform to the shape of the pole.

Sometimes figures are standing fully upright, but more often, they are crouching or sitting. Most creatures are shown facing the front, but animals such as the whale, dogfish, salmon and frog are shown as if seen from above and stretched facing up or down the pole. Smaller creatures may be coming from behind or inside the main figures and figures may overlap. Often it is the bottom figure that is the most important.

Wearable Cloth Art

Bill Helin

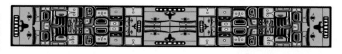

Chilkat Scarf

Going to the Potlatch

One traditional wearable artform was the fringed dancing blanket known as the Chilkat blanket. The blanket was made of mountain goat wool spun over a core of cedar-bark string.

The men hunted the goats, constructed the frame on which the weaving was done, and painted the design board for the women, who did the weaving, to use. Often representing an animal, the design was reordered and modified until it became abstract.

Representing the high point of weaving in Northwest Coast Native Art, these blankets were almost always black, white, yellow and blue. The design of the scarf pictured on this page is based on the Chilkat Blanket.

Today, much high fashion, ceremonial, and every-day clothing is being created by First Nations designers and artists and sold world-wide.

Creatures/Beings

In the aboriginal world of legends, there are many mythical or supernatural beings. Ordinary animals may have supernatural powers or spirit helper duties. This duality of worlds is often depicted in the art.

In this design, Wasgo, or Sea Wolf, is shown with the wolf head and tail of its counterpart in the natural world. It also has killer whale elements such as a dorsal fin. The claws are like flippers.

A spirit guide for fishers, it is related to undersea world beings like Sea Bear, Sea Raven, Sea Eagle, and Sea Frog. Sea Wolf may be one of those beings who carry the world on their backs.

Often, the heads of creatures are exaggerated in size and proportion. Some heads are as large as the bodies.

supernatural nostril

dorsal fin

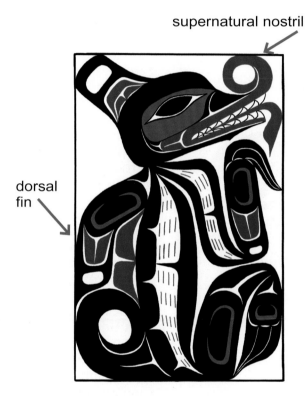

Wasgo the Sea Wolf

In the following pages, you will see beings that are two-dimensional and painted as in prints; the same creature in a line drawing that you might expect to see on engraved jewelry; and the same image as a three-dimensional carving, mask or totem pole figure.

Bear

North Coast Split Bear Design

Engraved Bear Head

Bears, so similar to humans as they stand on two legs, gather plants and berries, fish, and take care of their young, are frequently found in aboriginal art and legend.

Strong, fierce and devoted, bears are often depicted as guardians and protectors. They are the helping spirits of warriors. As well, they are a link between the earth and the spirit world.

Bearskin cloaks, teeth, and claws were, and still are, used in ceremony, ritual, and dance.

Associated with Bear is Bear Mother. The story varies from culture to culture, but it seems a high-ranking woman insulted Bear when she stepped in some bear dung while picking berries. After hearing about this insult, a Bear chief kidnaps and marries her. She gives birth to twin, magical cubs.

She and her children are later rescued by a relative and the human-bear children become the ancestors of the Bear Clan lineage.

You can identify a bear by its wide mouth, lips and teeth (usually sharp, often large canines), short, flat broad snout, often with round nostrils, short squared ears, large clawed feet which may be turned inward, tongue which often sticks out, and a small (or no) tail.

Bear Rattle

Bear Totem Pole Figure

Beaver

Beavers, hard-working and energetic, have excellent building skills, and provide plentiful food and shelter for their families.

Too busy to socialize, they keep separate from humans unless humans insult their skills or work. A natural disaster can be caused by one slap of a giant magic beaver's tail. When a beaver does decide to speak to a human, it gives wise advice, so it is best to listen.

North Coast Beaver

Silver Beaver Bracelet

Carved Beaver

Beaver, who is one of Raven's uncles, had his house, pond, berries, tools and all his salmon stolen by Raven.

Beaver is associated with many of the mythical creatures of the undersea world.

In the art, Beaver has a head like a bear except for the long, prominent front teeth; a short, wide, rounded snout; and a tail that is wide, flat, cross-hatched or has scales, and usually flips up in front of its body. Beaver is often holding a stick in its mouth or front paws. In addition to being a popular figure on poles, Beaver is often carved into a bowl, symbolizing his ability to provide.

Eagle

South Coast Eagle

Bill Helin

Eagle Bracelet

Eagles represent intelligence, peace, vigilance, and power, as well as superb vision. Many prominent clans have the eagle as ancestor. Powerful hunters, eagles represent healing, noble ideals, foresight and freedom. In many clans, eagle feathers and down are sacred. They are used in a variety of ceremonies and rituals, such as honouring respected guests, and healing the sick. Their down represents peace.

In the art, eagles are shown hunting whales in groups in order to be able to carry the heavy whale to shore. Eagles are often painted or carved with salmon, a favourite food, in their talons. They are also depicted with Raven.

Eagles have powerful downward curved beaks which may "recurve" or hook back toward the body. Usually there are no ears. Various U shapes represent wing and tail feathers, and talons.

Associated with eagles is Eagle Woman. Eagle Woman, unhappy in her marriage to Eagle, overcame dangerous obstacles to return with her two children to her own village. She swam a wide river by tying each child to her long braids, keeping her arms free. In this way, she became the clan mother of many human descendants.

Bill Helin

Eagle Orca Bracelet

Bill Helin

Eagle Totem Figure

Frog

Frogs, able to live in water and on land, are respected because they can adapt to many worlds, both earthly and spirit-filled. The knowledge and power of frogs make them primary spirit-helpers of shamans. They are considered to be great communicators; able to find mutual understanding in disputes or to speak for the common people.

Song is an important part of the aboriginal culture, and frog voice and song are believed to contain spiritual power. Also, the frog is associated with copper and prosperity.

Bill Helin

Frog and People

Frog Spoon Silver Pendant

In the art, Frog's tongue is often shown, representing sharing of knowledge and power. Frog faces can appear from other animals' ears, mouths, or hands. This may represent the other worlds to which Frog can travel.

You can tell a frog by its flat nose, broad mouth with no teeth, large round and often lidless eyes, short body, bent legs, no tail, no ears, and long, webbed toes.

Bill Helin

Frog

Human

**labret in
lower lip**

North Coast Woman

**Human Face
Engraved Pendant or Bracelet**

Families and ancestors are very important to the Northwest cultures. The ancestors are remembered at every gathering, and in human portraits in wood, paintings and precious metal. Sometimes a tree is is cut down and carved into a standing human figure that welcomes or guards.

Artists made tiny human amulets, dolls and puppets for play or ceremony. A shaman might use a figure in a ritual. The figure may represent a person, the sun, wind, a mountain, spirit or the important events in the human life cycle.

You can tell a human image because it usually has ears on the side of the head (or no ears), as opposed to animals which have ears on top of the head. Pouting or pursed lips may suggest that the image is singing, sucking, blowing, whistling, or talking. When

copper

Copper Chief

tongues are present, they may represent communication of shared knowledge and power, or an ability to understand different creatures. Pupils of eyes may show alertness, sleep, trance or death. Long hair represents power.

Artists may paint the face to show clan crests or status. Small animals painted or carved on the face might show the figure's spirit helpers.

There are wrinkled old-age masks, masks that show mourning, winking, and white men and women, representing the newly encountered European cultures.

The Copper is a shield-shaped symbol of wealth, power and status. Originally made of beaten copper, it was extremely valuable within the traditional economic system, worth many thousands of blankets. In the art, no matter what the material, this shape is called a Copper.

Orca (Killer Whale)

West Coast Orca

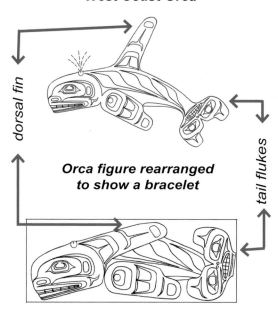

Orca figure rearranged to show a bracelet

dorsal fin

tail flukes

Killer whales or Orcas are seen as strong, dignified, prosperous and long-lived. Some cultures believe that the great chiefs have been reincarnated as Orcas. It is said that Killer Whales come close to shore to take the chief's spirit.

Orca spirits can also sink canoes and take their occupants to their villages under the sea. Killer Whale spirits may also guide people to safety.

Like wolves of the sea, Orcas are admired for their hunting skill, intelligence and devotion to family. Orca and wolves may be the same magical being, able to transform and adapt to land or sea.

When artists wish to show Orca as a supernatural being, there may be two, three or as many as five, dorsal fins.

You can identify an Orca by the large, long, rounded head; wide toothy mouth— often with canine teeth, blowhole, large dorsal fin, two small pectoral fins, and tail flukes. The smooth body is a modified ovoid. You can see it breaching or swimming. On poles, they may be seen lengthwise with head up or down.

Sometimes other creatures or spirits are found in the blowhole, flippers or body. Just a dorsal fin and blowhole with side flippers and tail or as little as a blowhole circle may represent the whole whale. A human may be riding on its back or a thunderbird may be holding Orca in its talons.

Bill Helin

Orca Wood Carving

Whale Dancer

Raven

North Coast Raven

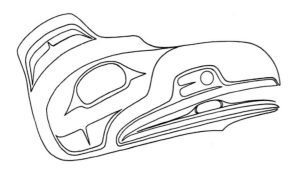

Engraved Raven Head

Tricky, cheeky, and exceptionally creative, Raven is one of the most important figures of Northwest Coast art and legend. We humans owe him gratitude for the gifts of fire, water, sun, moon, stars, and his discovery of humans and all other creatures.

Ruled by his curiosity and boundless appetites, he is the original organizer, transformer, teacher, and chief spirit under the Great Creator. His continual scheming to get whatever he wants, his practical jokes, lust, and impulsive nature get him into many uncomfortable situations. He is forced to be creative, using slyness, and trickery. He is never sorry or ashamed of what he does. He has the power to transform himself, other beings, plants and minerals.

Although Raven has the power of prophesy, he cannot

always tell when his own actions will get him into trouble. In stories, Raven, who is selfish, full of mischief and greedy, is also intelligent, innovative and resourceful.

In the art, Raven has a strong, straight tapering beak. Sometimes, the tip is slightly curved or squared. On the head, there are short ears or no ears, and the wings are often folded against the black-painted body.

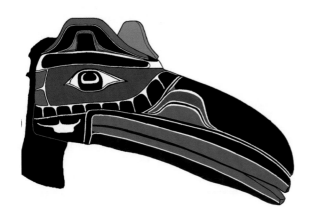

Mid Coast Raven Mask

Raven`s Tales

Salmon

Mid Coast Salmon

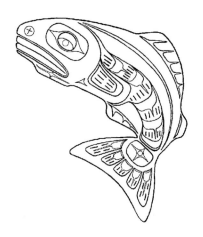

Salmon from the West Coast

A crucial source of food, salmon are honoured and celebrated in ritual and ceremony by all coastal tribes. When the salmon is shown in the art, it symbolizes the eternal cycle of life and the salmon's self-sacrifice, and perseverance.

If the salmon were not plentiful one year, it was said to be due to disrespect by the people. Perhaps they had refused to listen to and live by traditional wisdom.

It was important to welcome the first salmon and to place all of the salmon's bones back into the rivers or into the sea after eating or they wouldn't return.

Shamans or chiefs might go to the salmon villages under the sea and learn how to help their people survive and prosper.

In some regions, women had high status and were greatly respected. Women were essential in the salmon economy. Their skills and work as they prepared and preserved the salmon was as important as catching it. The job of making sure the food source would last and keeping it safe long after the salmon season meant the survival of the people.

You can tell a salmon by its short fins, round eyes, down-turned mouth, sometimes hooked mouth (of a spawning salmon), long body, and typical fish gills, scales and tail. Salmon are often carved in pairs because they are the spirit guides for twins.

Bill Helin

down-turned mouth, hooked

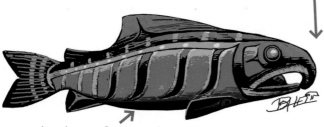

red colour of spawning

Spawning Salmon

Sea Lion

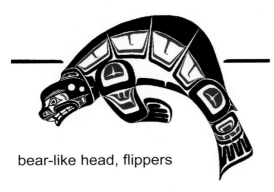

bear-like head, flippers

Mid Coast Sea Lion

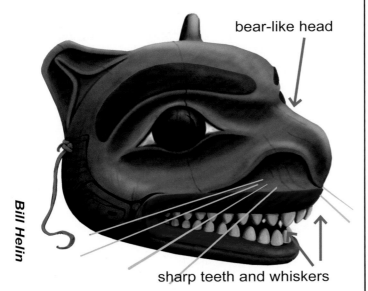

bear-like head

Bill Helin

sharp teeth and whiskers

Sea Lion Mask

In the world of legend, Sea Lions are the head guards at the house of the Chief of the Undersea World. Sea Lions are often seen as house posts in the great community houses of some tribes.

In the art, Sea Lion has a head like a bear; a rounded snout with whiskers; short, often sharp, teeth; small ears; a thick body; and flippers at the sides and/or rear. Generally, a sea lion is shown with teeth but seals are not.

Sea Otter

Mid Coast Sea Otter and Pup

otters floating on their backs, holding with their paws

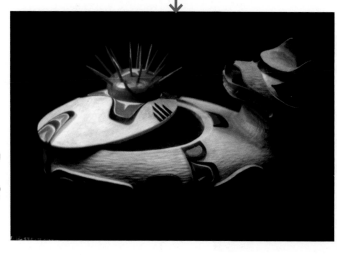

Ron Stacy

Sea Otter and Sea Urchin Bowl

The sea otter was challenging to hunt and its pelt was highly prized after contact. Pelts brought wealth in trade. Intelligent, resourceful, and nimble, otters use their forepaws like hands.

Because they are so playful, they symbolize laughter, lightheartedness and play.

Sea Otter is shown with a long streamlined body, often swimming. It has a long thick tail, small ears, wide eyes, and rounded head with a short snout. Otter's strong mouth often has sharp teeth. It is traditionally shown on its back holding a shell, sea urchin or fish.

In the north, it was Land Otter who had the knowledge and power of otters and humans. Hunters were forbidden to kill land otters.

Shark (Dogfish)

body split into
halves showing
x-ray of insides

high domed head

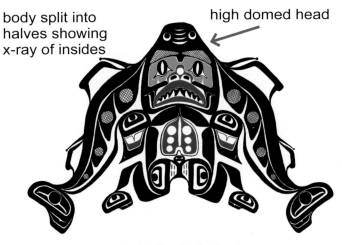

Split Dogfish Design

hooked beak nose and triangular teeth

Bill Helin

Dogfish Gold Bracelet

The Dogfish is an important crest and mythical being. This shark usually swims alone and is respected and even feared.

In the art, dogfish images have high domed heads that represent the fish's snout. The mouth turns down and has the typical sharp triangular teeth of a shark. The large eyes usually have oval pupils. Gills can be found in the cheeks and the top of the head. Some designs have a nose like a hooked beak. The large tail flukes are not symmetrical just as in real life.

Every-day objects often carry a Dogfish crest. The Dogfish is able to enter the Realm of the Supernatural. It is also one of the most powerful crests associated with feminine qualities.

A being associated with this crest is Dogfish Woman. She is often portrayed with a labret in her lower lip as a reminder of the legend of the woman carried off by the Dogfish a long time ago. The labret in her lower lip is traditionally worn by high-ranking Northwest Coast women.

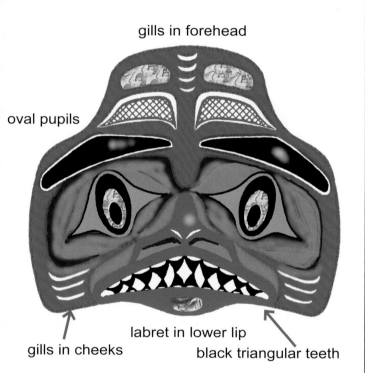

gills in forehead

oval pupils

gills in cheeks

labret in lower lip

black triangular teeth

North Coast Dogfish Woman Mask

Sisiutl

two wolf-like serpent heads with middle head

supernatural curly horns and nostrils

Mid Coast Sisiutl

two serpent heads turned toward middle head

Bill Helin

Sisiutl Bracelet

Bill Helin

Embossed Sisiutl

Sisiutl, a frightening, powerful, double-headed sea serpent, guards the house of the sky family. The two heads symbolize the two sides of its nature; it can destroy but it can also give power. Able to transform into a fish or a self-propelled canoe, one look can kill or turn an enemy to stone.

On the other hand, it is also a spirit guide who is able to make warriors powerful and invulnerable. Sometimes warriors wore a headband and belt with the Sisiutl design. If you should net or hook a Sisiutl, throw sand on it, be careful not to touch it directly, tie it tightly, and never take it into your house. If you keep it in water and then wash in the resulting medicine-water, it will bring you health and long life.

The Sisiutl is usually shown horizontally, or arched, or in a circle as a double-headed serpent, two wolf-like heads at each end with long tongues and curly horns. There is a human-like face with two curly horns in the middle. Curly horns always indicate a supernatural creature as do flared/curled nostrils.

'Namgis First Nation Sisiutl Welcome Sign at Alert Bay, Canada

Sun

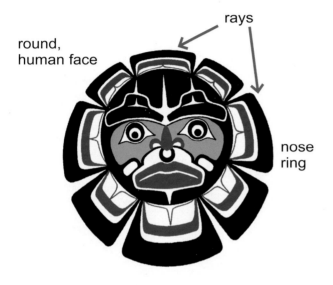

round,
human face

rays

nose
ring

Moon

no
rays

labret in
lower lip

Round-faced Sun, with its ability to give life by supplying energy in the form of heat and light, also has the potential to destroy that same life by scorching and killing.

Also round-faced, Moon is not usually shown with rays. Moon, also a protector and guardian spirit, is connected with transformation. Moon can be male or, more commonly, female.

In the image shown, the labret in the lower lip indicates a female. Sometimes the Moon is linked to wolves, creatures of the night. Often, Moon is found in Raven's long beak, part of the story of how Raven stole the light from its imprisoning box and released it to humans as the sun, moon and stars.

In legend, the Sun often acts as a benevolent spirit guide.

You can tell the Sun by its round face with any number of rays surrounding it, or at least the suggestion of rays. Rays may be shown as hands, which symbolize the gifts of creativity and generosity given by the Sun. The faces vary, sometimes human, other times like an Eagle or Raven. The Sun, most commonly male, and shown with a nose ring on the opposite page, can also be female.

rays

hooked beak-like nose

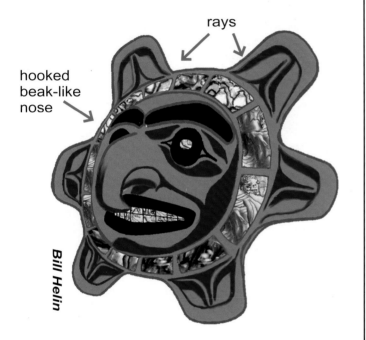

Bill Helin

Carved Sun

Thunderbird

curly ears or horns

outstretched wings

lightning snake

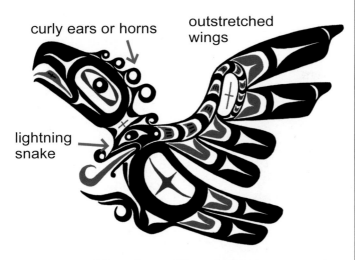

West Coast Thunderbird

North Coast Thunderbird

Thunderbird, esteemed ancestor of many human lineages, is a giant, supernatural bird named because he causes lightning and thunder. When he flaps his wings, thunder booms. When he blinks his majestic eyes or throws his Lightning Snakes, lightning flashes. He is intelligent and proud, and not often outwitted by humans.

You can tell him by his powerful hooked beak. On his head are large often curly ears, horns or head appendages, always indicating supernatural power. He has large legs and talons, large outstretched or folded wings. Thunderbird often has a longer beak than Eagle.

Often, Thunderbird is shown with Killer Whale in his talons.

curly ears or horns

strong curved beak

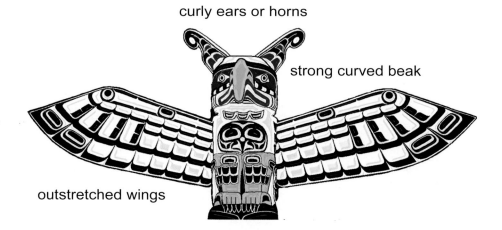

outstretched wings

Thunderbird Totem Figure from the Mid Coast

Lightning Snake

Lightning Snake is a feathered serpent, a powerful sea monster with a head like a wolf and a long tongue. The embodiment of lightning, two snakes are usually carried under Thunderbird's enormous wings. The thunderbird hunts whales, using his Lightning Snakes to pierce and wound the whale until it is helpless.

West Coast
Lightning Snake

Wild Man of the Woods - Bukwus

forest colours   cedar bark hair

Bill Helin

hooked nose

fierce scowling mouth

Bakwas mask

Bukwus, Bakwas, Bookwee, or Wild Man of the Woods, waits at the edge of the forest near the streams. He hopes that the unlucky soul of a drowned person might eat his offered ghost food and cross to the Spirit World to join him and be just like him. Children are taught to be wary and not go alone into the woods and near water to avoid meeting those discontented spirits doomed to eternal hunger, misery, and wandering.

You can identify him by his hollow cheeks, hooked or beak-like nose, large fierce mouth with or without teeth. There may be twigs, branches or cedar bark hair. He is usually painted with forest colours like green, brown and black.

Wild Woman of the Woods - Dzunukwa

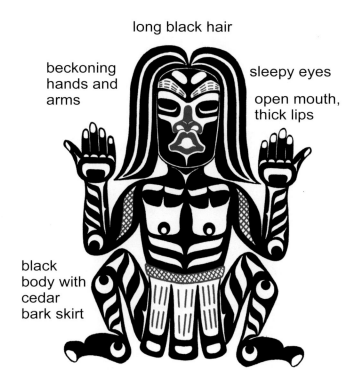

long black hair

beckoning hands and arms

sleepy eyes

open mouth, thick lips

black body with cedar bark skirt

Mid Coast Wild Woman of the Woods

Known also as Tsonoqua, this female monster is giant, hairy, and often shown with a beard. Sometimes she has wide eyes or sleepy eyes. Her body is black with big breasts. Her thick lips, and open mouth shout "hooo, hooo" with a supernatural thunderous voice. She is supernaturally strong and magical. She has great wealth, eats humans, and travels underground. She is responsible for her children, the creatures and spirits of the forest.

If she should capture a human child, she may be tricked into letting the child escape from the basket on her back. She can be tricked out of her wealth or can bestow it on a clever human.

Humans must beware of the upthrust hands and outstretched arms. She is dangerous, not welcoming.

Wolf

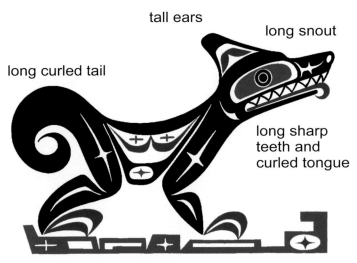

tall ears

long snout

long curled tail

long sharp teeth and curled tongue

West Coast Wolf

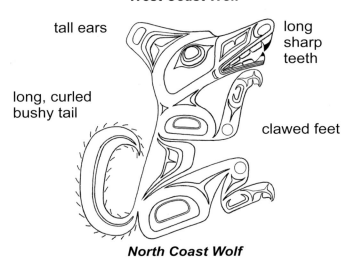

tall ears

long sharp teeth

long, curled bushy tail

clawed feet

North Coast Wolf

Wolves, with their eerie howls, barks, and yelping as they communicate, are respected for strength, agility, intelligence, and devotion to family. The impressive language of wolves matches the aboriginal peoples' belief in the power of speech and song to transform and make magic. Some cultures believe that Wolf, associated with whales in legend taught men the secrets of whale hunting.

You can recognize a Wolf by its long snout with nostrils, long sharp teeth with prominent fangs, tall narrow ears, ovoid eyes, clawed feet, and long curled and/or bushy tail. Sometimes, the tongue sticks out and often curls upward or downward symbolizing communication.

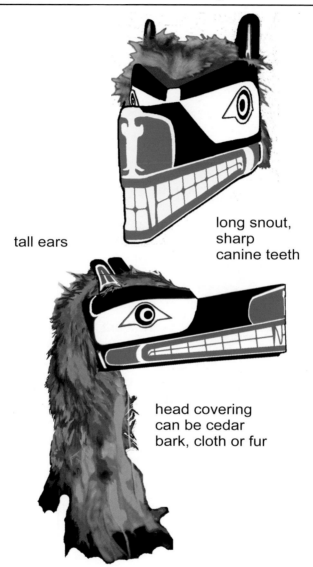

tall ears

long snout,
sharp
canine teeth

head covering
can be cedar
bark, cloth or fur

Mid Coast Wolf Mask

Design Components

At the time of European contact, painted designs were found on North and Mid Coast house fronts, boxes, chests, canoes, paddles, dance screens, masks, helmets, hats, drums, rattles, ceremonial regalia, seats, coppers and clothing. In the South Coast, house posts and grave figures were painted.

Formline

A formline is a continuous, curving line which swells and shrinks in width throughout its length, seldom becoming parallel with other lines and delineating a form or a shape.

See **Other Shapes** on page 62 for a full explanation of the relieving shapes pictured here.

All images in this section are by Jim Gilbert

Relieving Shapes

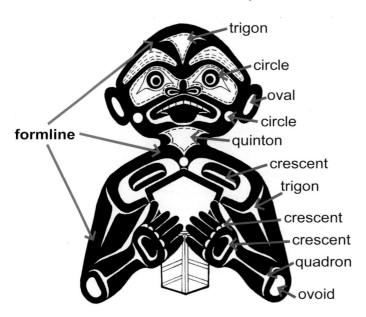

trigon
circle
oval
circle
quinton
crescent
trigon
crescent
crescent
quadron
ovoid

formline

Man with Copper

Ovoid

Pacific Skate Photo

Salmon egg and salmon egg resting on a stream bed.

Ovoid outline

North Coast spiny sea urchin

South Coast style Ovoid - rounder

North Coast style Ovoid - wider at the top

Mid Coast style Ovoid - wider at the bottom

Looking a little like a jelly bean or loaf of bread, an ovoid can vary from a near circle to a shallow, elongated, rectangle with rounded corners. Although some ovoid shapes are more common in one area than another, many styles and shapes may be found within the same design, according to the artist's choice,

Where did the shape come from? Perhaps the ovoid comes from the markings on the pectoral fins (wings) of the Pacific big skates, or the shell profile of a sea urchin. Still others suggest that the pad prints of the salmon-loving bear or even the resting salmon eggs themselves, when viewed in profile, have the basic outline shape of an ovoid.

Ovoids can represent heads, bodies, feet, paws, ears, tails, fins or any number of other creatures or things.

U shape

Shaped like the letter "U", U shapes can be lengthened, shortened, inverted or rotated in a design in order to represent cheeks, ears, nostrils, mouths, arms, legs, toes, wings, and joined to represent lips, fins, feathers, tail flukes, fingers, claws, paws, and tails.

Solid blocks of colour may be split into two mirrored halves. They are usually black formlines with red interiors. U shapes can contain textures like crosshatching, lines or dashing. Crosshatching is often black but there can be red crosshatching within a black formline.

U shape with fineline split

U shape with wider bottom and tapering legs

U shape with inner reverse split

U shape with inner solid split

U shape representing a killer whale's dorsal fin with dashing, and crosshatching

S Shape

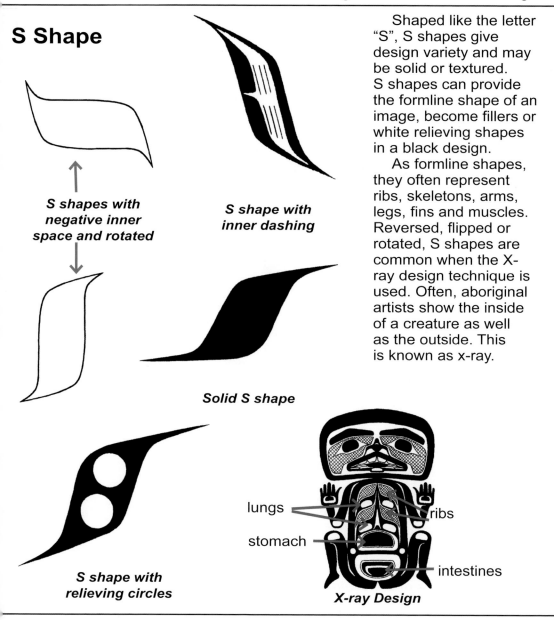

Shaped like the letter "S", S shapes give design variety and may be solid or textured. S shapes can provide the formline shape of an image, become fillers or white relieving shapes in a black design.

As formline shapes, they often represent ribs, skeletons, arms, legs, fins and muscles. Reversed, flipped or rotated, S shapes are common when the X-ray design technique is used. Often, aboriginal artists show the inside of a creature as well as the outside. This is known as x-ray.

S shapes with negative inner space and rotated

S shape with inner dashing

Solid S shape

lungs

stomach

ribs

intestines

S shape with relieving circles

X-ray Design

Box End Design

Designs that are a combination of U shapes and ovoids are often found on the ends of bentwood boxes.

The U shapes may be found attached to the sides of the ovoid or to the top and bottom. Connections are usually done very smoothly with a fine line or overlapped to show a negative space, such as a trigon, as a separator. (See page 62)

Box end design with U shapes attached to the top and bottom of the ovoid salmon head

Box end design with U shapes attached to the sides of the ovoid salmon head

Salmon Head Design

Salmon head with teeth

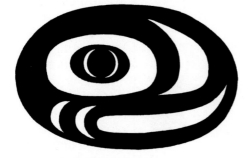

Salmon head from the south coast

Salmon head from the west coast of Vancouver Island

Although salmon head design units vary greatly in shape and complexity, all salmon heads have a black eyeball and eyelid line and a snout/nose. If there is a mouth or jaw, it may be empty or contain teeth and/or a tongue. A cheek design often appears at the rear of the mouth.

Also known as salmon-trout heads, salmon heads are often found in eyeballs, joints, or box end designs.

Other Shapes

Circle with crescent relieving shape

Circle with trigon relieving shape

Circle with quadron relieving shape

Neck area with quinton relieving shape

U shape ear containing human head

Trigon
This shape is a closed negative design element with three curved sides and three points, often seen as T or Y shaped. It delineates or helps outline shapes in a design.

Quadron
This shape is a closed figure with four curved sides and four points, usually negative, that delineates or helps outline the shapes in a design.

Quinton
This shape is a closed figure with five curved sides and five points, usually negative, that delineates or helps outline shapes in a design.

Available from Raven Publishing Inc.

Learning by Doing Northwest Coast Native Indian Art
by Karin Clark and Jim Gilbert ISBN 0-9692979-1-2
- step-by-step instructions and illustrations on the basics of drawing, designing, painting and carving
- over 300 black and white detailed illustrations and 32 photos, soft cover, 160 pages

Learning by Designing Pacific Northwest Coast Native Indian Art, Volume 1   by Jim Gilbert and Karin Clark ISBN 0-9692979-3-9
- detailed, thoroughly analyzed, well-supported comparison of the four Pacific Northwest First Nations art styles
- 800 clear, black and white detailed illustrations, soft cover, 244 pages

Learning by Designing Pacific Northwest Coast Native Indian Art, Volume 2   by Jim Gilbert and Karin Clark ISBN 0-9692979-4-7
- full colour, 16-page creation story with 20 designs
- 20 designs to draw and paint,
- over 100 designs in a Quick Reference Chart
- Native Indian philosophy, code of ethics, and interviews
- Soft cover, 176 pages

In the Beginning, There was the First World by Jim Gilbert, Ron Stacy and Wedlidi Speck ISBN 0-9692979-5-5
- full-colour, 16-page booklet is included in our Learning by Designing, Volume 2, book.
- beautifully illustrated Pacific Northwest Coast creation story as well as 20 designs from the four major Native Indian art style areas

Cross Stitch Patterns Based on Pacific Northwest Coast Native Indian Art Styles: Book 1 Thunderbirds by Jim Gilbert & Sheron Ruffell
ISBN 0-9692979-7-1
- The first of a series, this book contains the three full-size colour cross stitch patterns from the West, Mid, and North Coast shown on the front cover.
- Patterns are approximately 37 cm x 27 cm (14"x11") with each based on accurate, traditional designs.

Bill Helin

Potlatch at the Crossroads of Time

Acknowledgments

My deep appreciation to artists Jim Gilbert, Bill Helin (www.billhelin.com), and Ron Stacy (www.stacystudios) for their contributions and support of me as a writer and struggling artist.

To:

Bruce Jolliffe, Georgina Jolliffe, Jeneen Karsch, Ron Stacy;

Pamela Mitchell and Samantha Christiansen from the I-Hos Gallery in Comox;

Maureen Gouliquer from the Wei Wai Kum House of Treasures in Campbell River;

Nella Nelson, co-ordinator of the Aboriginal Nations Education Division of the Greater Victoria School District;

my sincere thanks for the many hours of editing work and the great suggestions.

Thank you to Maria Rey for translating the book into German.